A Man's House Catches Fire

A Man's House Catches Fire

Tom Sastry

Nine
Arches
Press

A Man's House Catches Fire
Tom Sastry

ISBN: 978-1911027744
eBook ISBN: 978-1911027843

Cover artwork: 'House on Fire' © Becca Stadtlander, courtesy of Bright Art Licensing. www.beccastadtlander.com

Published October 2019 by:

Nine Arches Press
Unit 14, Sir Frank Whittle Business Centre,
Great Central Way, Rugby.
CV21 3XH
United Kingdom

www.ninearchespress.com

Nine Arches Press is supported using public funding by Arts Council England.

Contents

When the light reminds you to look

Misenchantment

A man's house catches fire

I was suddenly uncomfortably hot
but I have always had these surges, and at first
I thought the smell of smoke
was just me going off my head

which I have learnt to expect.
I closed the curtains, undressed
turned the heating off and lay
in the last of my stillness

watching the shadow of a flame
playing on the wall
until the shadow reddened
and I could see no way out.

It's been a month now
with the fire still raging
and me not dead
and no help coming

so today I stepped outside
smelling more than ever of myself.
My oldest friend was passing.
She said *Is it that time?*

Are the houses of men burning too?
I said *You're mistaken.*
Nothing is burning.
and I stepped back into my house.

Thirty-two lines on loss

Everywhere, they are selling:
the sun in orange juice; the sex
in perfume; thirty pence from a box
of fishfingers, tasting of sea. I lost

my glasses. I left them on the table
in the café because I was tired of looking
at billboards and wanted some thoughts
of my own and because I liked the fog of it

but when I went to leave, they were gone.
It was Sunday and the opticians
were closed. I soon realised the world
is full of monsters travelling too fast.

One of these is time. I spent a lot of time sitting that day.
I drank a lot of coffee because that is what I do
when I sit. Perhaps I drank too much.
I did a lot of thinking

and I wanted it to last longer. But the sun set
and the sun rose and I called in sick
and got some new glasses. They filmed me
in the frames. I looked like a total dick

staring straight ahead like the world's
toothiest convict. You always do.
You accept it. They said it would take an hour
to make them up, so I went out

into the fog and found a café. I just killed time
and checked my phone. When I went to go
I couldn't get up. My body was a sandbag.
I cried like a doll. I must have really hated the idea

of functioning again. I hated it so much.
I hated it so much that for a moment
the surprise of how much I hated it
stopped everything, even the hate.

The birds are leaving

God knows for where
but they are mustering
on each gutter and tile
calling down wires
lobbing news from gable to gutter
fussing grimly with the project of it
checking feathers
and reading the wind from rumour.

The birds are churching together
summoning their luck
sharing the last good scavenging days
breathing the last of the old smoke.

They have their drummers.
They have their badges and colours.
They call out
the who and the where and the when –
you cannot call it a song –
before rising like a tent
rasping the air with their din.

There is a sudden hush, then
a cacophonous beating of wings.

The sky remains lost.

The importance of not listening (1)

Death is coming says the sticker
(black bold on lilac, no border).

I only saw it because I was on the top deck
thinking about the worst thing I have ever done
whether it is worse than things people go to prison for

what it means to be worse
and what it means to be forgiven.

Then I started wondering why
someone would plant a thought like that
eight feet up, on the brow of the bus shelter

and that's how it got into my head
that I might need to worry.

Underground

The dead pass through turnstiles into the earth.

They glide down into tiled halls
or seek out the forgotten steps
that spill out onto the shore
of the thin black river.

They stand on the jetty
bothered by hot winds
and stare into the dark mouth of time.

Posters convince them that where they're going
they need whiskey and economic news.

The smash-irons of ghost factories
chant in the darkness like choirs.

Then they emerge, solitary, unchanged;
dragging their cases past the unimagined knees
of strangers; eyes pointing towards
the next crossing, the next coffee;
tongues coated in benzene and mint;
ears full of music, hands full of news.

The museum of regret

You carry your takeaway cup
in the hand your daughter wanted.
The clock is too loud.

A woman sells strips of balsa wood.
The price is ten minutes.
You kneel with her, as Jesus would

then draw pins from your knees
and make crosses
for the little shrines. Later

you leave smeared prints on the glass
over the balled letters
and worn-out brakes.

It is Memory Day. They open the cabinets
to let the time in.
Something older than dust

jumps at the chance of an honest throat.
You ignore the cough.
Two mannequins

turn their heads to face
each other, then turn away.
Your office phone rings

you hear it singing
your mother's invitation, your lover's weekend
the last of the afternoon.

The office

Keyboards slork and chirrup their way
through diets of words. The striped cough of the printer
punctuates the settling of sludge-mugs
on woodskim tops. Everything has its secret grammar.
Voices skit and burr on phatic tides,
the cobbler's thumb imprints the damped floor
and a phone makes the sound

of a bird. I don't know which one. We do not have names
for birds in here. You can bring the name of a bird
in from outside, if you like. You can bring its call
on your ringtone, you can bring
the possibility of a bird. You can bring it on the chance
of a call from your letting agent or lover.
It can trill in your pocket. No-one will mind.

The souls of the dead await judgement

The room is white as a page.
We don't touch. Perhaps we can't.
We have that airport sadness.

The first time they called out the numbers
people clutched their tickets and surged forward.
After that, they took down the clock.

In the face of so much boredom
we have created service industries.
For three blinks, I will blow on your hand.

People get to the front of the line.
You smile at them, make them feel something.
Before long, it becomes work.

Your heart is a servant you keep in a cage

Alan walked away from his job.
It was the new people treating each thing he said
as a little joke they were good enough not to rise to.
It hurt him so much that he went, alone
into the darkness without mythology
working for the nightly use of his friend's sofa
living at the frayed edge of his friend's politeness

and some of us missed him

so we gathered, spoke his name
sighed, shook our heads, agreed he should have
sat tight, tried to get a transfer
looked for something else, made them pay him off
until someone said
that maybe he *loved* his job
which is absurd because no-one does
but it would explain
why he needed to erase himself

because your heart is a servant you keep in a cage
for its relentless nature
until one day
it finds a way
to break you.

Heart

How old is your heart?
asks Public Health England:
an irresistible question.

Who wants a plate-glass heart
unfrosted by history?
Who wants a leaping

uncynical heart;
a tone-deaf, click-track heart
feeding the flush of their round face?

I want my old shabby heart
the same way I want, one day
to live in the woods: me

who can hardly live in town
who finds living very hard
who is tired of persisting.

Misenchantment

(noun)

1. The exact amount of fear required
to beautify a lonely place at night;

2. a voluntary absence from the body;

3. the desire not to return;

4. the desire to live underwater;

5. the letterbox and its hanging tongue of bills;

6. the music of inkwater at the lip of the moony pool;

7. an obsession with the undersides of things;

8. the view of lilypads from below.

Voiceover for an advert for modern life

Imagine that exile was the thing you were born for.

Imagine being lonely without shame.

Imagine ready meals that taste of indulgence; imagine all the time
you can eat.

Imagine privacy.

Imagine a bus whose passengers don't pretend to have anywhere to go.

Imagine a world of sound with the texture of silence, free from
human noise.

Imagine the library hush of a busy office.

Imagine ceiling tiles.

Imagine trees and cars; cars and trees.

Imagine birds, as if for the first time.

Imagine never coming home; imagine never having left.

Simple magic for dark times

Try to see clearly what it is you love.
Whatever you love, be honest.
If it is your family, more than the world
do not be ashamed.
If it is your cat
or the smother of the morning bed
or a certain goal scored at Wembley in the 1970s
have no regrets.
Be proud of your love.
Bring it to mind. Bring it to the front
ahead of all other concerns.
It is hard to do but not impossible.
Hold it, as literally as you can, in your hands.
It is touching you. Touch it back.
Say goodbye.
You need to get it out of the country.
You need to preserve it.
Write it, draw it, pickle it, cure it
freeze it, hide it, bury it
put it in a bottle
tell it to a friend
carry it in the hollow sole of an old shoe
to wherever it will be safe.

When hope has bolted
into the deepest cave of your belly
hiding from all the temporary things
the memory of your love will have a form
and you can summon it –

when its lightness feels like an insult
when you need it most.

The unheroic

A man learns to live with fire

I fed my life to the fire but it wasn't hungry.
The smoke crossed out the air
but was somehow breathable.

Sometimes I placed a hand and took a burn
but mostly the fire was content
to be feared

and I, obediently, feared it –
wearing wet clothes night and day
taking the flames at a blind dash.

I had never lived at the pleasure
of an emergency that doesn't stop:
an illness, a tyrant, a God.

I had to learn to carry the feeling
like a stone in my head
that sometimes remembers it is molten.

I came to know it
as my endurance
my aftermath.

There was no-one else
to embody it.
It was mine.

Normalisation

It's like the old days; a fortnight's needs
in tins under the stairs. The crisis
like the weather, is changeable. Some days
the shops are full, the power constant.
Some days the streets are calm. The news is still
earnest nothings, outrage, sport and gossip.
They haven't yet asked for your passwords.
The leaves turn. You still have a job.

The wild existence the hippies wanted
is here. We are a tribe with toasters.
We sing to the fire. People listen more
to the world beyond words, feel the warm gift
of fragile bodies. Keep Your Head Down
as the slogan says. Then Hold It High.

The importance of not listening (2)

Do not listen to the sea.
It contains the consequences
of everything you have done.

Do not listen to the sea.
It hides plastics
and weapons of mass destruction.

Do not listen to the sea.
It's Halloween down there
full of dark and bones.

Do not listen to the sea.
Isn't life hard enough?
None of this is your fault.

Do not listen to the sea.
Build a wall on every beach.
Sing patriotic songs.

Complicity

No-one knows where the clowns went.
Perhaps they found their own country.
Perhaps they were frightened.

Look –

there's a boy in Weston-Super-Mare
who says he saw, lined up on the mud at low tide
small piles of braces, red wigs
bellied pantaloons and oversized shoes.

The great marquees of England stand empty
and somewhere
a melancholy lion licks an abandoned red nose
while children fall over the guy ropes
with *look-at-me* smiles.

The politicians are explaining.
If they have left says the PM
it was their choice.
I myself am the son of clowns.
We just wanted to disperse them
to prevent them from clustering together
in ghettoes.

It's not just him.
No-one says they feel guilty. There's just this

nostalgia. There are record downloads
of classic bike horn and ukulele tunes.
New museums are planned.
The Commission on Nightmares
has proposed a new terror of badgers
but we all know it won't be the same.

We do our best to remember.
Last night, a group of us
sniffed trick roses on the bandstand
and wiped our dripping faces
smudging our greasepaint smiles.

Goldilocks

Everyone loved the wild girl. She meant
what we wanted her to mean. She cartwheeled
out of the forest like a ribbon, dirt on the bones
of her face; she screamed and bit, then washed
and smiled and played the piano. She said

that in a house a mile from the track
there were bears. She said she ran from the house
and now wakes in the night, trembling. She said this house
was a cave of secrets, hidden in a nightmare
not far from here. What else could we do? –

we walked, a long line of women and men,
reporters and dogs, into the night of the wild girl
with our axes and our noses and our lifetime's rage.
We walked into the forest with our questions
looking for the house a mile from the track

where the bears live. We found the sun sliding down
the roof; we found the blinds down. What more proof
could there be? A hero struck the door
with the handle of his axe. Silence. His strong voice said
We are the people! It was all done well. We knew

the bears had the advantage. We couldn't see them
so we fell upon the house as one. No-one said
Charge! We were singing. We were parts of a body
that adored itself. We were frightened together.
We loved each other. We never found

the bears. But there were bones in the ash we left:
the skull of a child we were too late to save;
charred pieces of a man, perhaps a woman too.
Now, on Sundays, we ride our boots back out
into the wild girl's night. The hunt goes on.

Jeremy Paxman interviews the old woman who lives in the woods

I asked about the children and she said
what children?

I asked about the children and she said it was *very worrying.*

I asked about the children and she said
a boy and a girl, very polite

I asked about the children and she said
who was watching them?

I asked about the children and she said
they cried for their father

I asked about the children and she said
skin and bone

I asked about the children. She said she gave them food
made sure they were warm.

I asked about the children and she said
this isn't about the children

I asked about the children and she said
an old woman in the woods
with only her hands
doors barred to her
dogs set on her

I asked about the children.
She vanished in a puff of spit.
A fox met my eye and screamed.
A young woman and a young man came out of the house.
The young woman picked up the fox.
It touched her cheek with its cheek.
The young man gave me a cup of sweet tea.

I asked about the children.
A parrot rose in my throat
and the only the thing it knew how to say
was *possibly, maybe, perhaps.*

Without the knowledge of her superiors

The bird, stiff, pinched between finger and thumb
drops into the food waste.

Somewhere, in the parliament of your conscience
a spokesman for a party

which denies direct links to your cat
calls it *A tragedy*.

At the next blink, you remember the eye
tilted to meet yours by the neck's unfortunate curve.

It was yellow-green, the colour of young wine.
Not beady, just a bead.

The feathers you sweep deny gravity.
They ride on a carpet of your breath

and settle in the unreachable corners of your day.
At the foot of the stairs, where she left the spoil

the culprit waits. You call her by name.
She howls like a bereaved lover. You are loyal.

Whatever is said, you will not give her up.
At least this is nature, not death

machined into a packet. You tell her
to lie low for a few days. She yawns

showing the depths of her appetite,
her boastful teeth. She remains capable.

The Russians

Yes. It's a real un-made-up fact.
The Russians sent a dog into space
to see what would happen. She says in that case
the Russians are evil. That's how
the cold war starts. I say I don't believe
in evil, and she says
they should send criminals instead
of innocent dogs. I say
But what if the dog had bitten someone?

She knows I'm mocking her.
It sounds cruel now, but imagine:
it's 1986, missiles pointing everywhere.
She wants to go to war over a dog.
She thinks people who don't love dogs
are monsters. She knows I fear racism:
she hates whole countries. She won't see it.
So I do a brave thing. I laugh in her face
while she cries. I'm young.
I can't let it go.

In the third year of National Renewal

we listed unaltered facts
(the height of the tor, the shitty weather)

extravagantly loved our small view
of the dark heaven, our familiar streets

taught our children to believe
that nothing was wrong

returned to the forgotten lanes of our lives
laid new hopes on those old dead ends

outraged each other over trifles
so we could scream

moved to the country
made our own wine

immersed ourselves in soap operas
and seasons of sport

meditated, had affairs
handed in our keys, our jobs

grew lines on our bodies
avoided hospitals

considered politics
as just another cause of death

(a tiny risk
a rounding error)

used words precisely
so as to mean nothing.

When, in their dangerous messages
the exiles dreamed loudly

we imagined their hopes for us
and hated them, without prompting.

We are drowning. Everyone else is Noah.

Somewhere
               on the inaccessible side of the u-bend
an apprentice fatberg achieves total coverage of the pipe.

The house cannot pass water. The courtyard fills.

Our modern life ends.
                    We bail ten gallons a time
into the trug and carry it, writhing
out the front door.

At first, we wait until the street is quiet
before swilling our effluent down the hill.

We're soon past caring.

We give up our hurried strip-washes and stop cooking.
We order sixty sandbags.

From the upstairs window
we hear the neighbours get into their car
making the joke about cholera
we made days ago
                  but enjoyed less.

And still the rain, the incessant rain.

I join a gym for the showers and linger
doughy and myopic in the cleansing warmth
next to clear-eyed, rock-bellied gods.

I am full of hate for everyone.
I am more polite than I have ever been.

We move our precious things upstairs
and tape over the plug sockets.
Plumbers' voicemails promise
to consider outdoor jobs when the rain stops.

           It doesn't.

On the fortieth day we lie on our bed and let the water erase us.

A city of static arks
warns itself against our fatal sins.

Its doves bleat triumphantly.
Its plumbers turn their phones back on.

The unheroic

On the internet, news and cricket
are the same: a predictable succession
of slow explosions, where the end result
is more play tomorrow. The sunrise
will not arrive for everyone
but it will arrive. Perhaps one day
England will lose by an impossible margin –
an innings and a thousand.
Shoe sizes will change, money
show different faces, cars swap sides.
More likely, the first revolution I see
will be my own death and until then
I will tune in and out of a crisis that never ends –
government chaos, run on the pound,
benefit sanctions, deportations.
Of course it's bad: one hundred and thirty
for six at lunch: a lead of just
fifty-one. But one thing follows another
at least for now: lungs fill
and fill again;
this time with effort, *this time* with feeling
always to the rhythm of *this time*.

The state mortician

At this moment, the President is both dead
and alive. It's true that armed men
are watching me undress a corpse
but it could just be a rehearsal.

What is said on CNN may be lies
and in any case, *elements which parrot*
the foreign media are not representative
of the people. Just now, on state television

the President addressed the graduates
of the Institute of Policing
on the subject of *Threats to Civil Peace.*
He was clearly in excellent health.

I have work to do.
I begin by closing his eyes.

Sweet Biscuit Man

if you aren't lost / you will be a museum piece / rare and therefore
beautiful / like a stuffed dodo / or a megalith

your voice notes will be valuable / a thousand irreplaceable mouthfuls
/ of long-dead language

your body will be precious /a leather bag of relics

your £7 daysack / will be carefully unzipped / by latex-covered hands
for its trove / of receipts / biros / and small packets of convenience food

your cloth cap will not be / "read" / as ironic

you will be given a name you wouldn't recognise / Sodbury Woman
or Sweet Biscuit Man

the remains of your last meal will prove / you had access to bananas and
poppy seeds / they will assume you were high / a priest of some sort

perhaps they already know / from adverts / that white people couldn't
stop embracing you / as you walked down the street

to prevent further misunderstandings / you could carve notes /
on non-biodegradable plastic

saying in various ways / how you wanted things to be different /
but also / to love them as they were

or you could just / walk blindly into the future / like there's any choice

hold on to this / time erodes all meanings / it's OK

When the light reminds you to look

Man and fire move house

It is the most deliberately violent thing I have done –
punching whatever came to hand
deep into the belly of a black sack

until all that was left
were moths of paper
and rovings of lint.

I hunted them down
throttle-tied the bags
drove to the dump and hurled the lot over the wall.

Then I glanced down at a whole city's
most furiously forgotten things
to see how monsters die

as old junk.
One thing remained. I tilted my head.
An old inferno dropped from my ear onto my palm

a hot plug of tar
round as an eyeball
red ribbons swimming on its surface.

My reckless fingertips explored its texture
noticed it was cooling.
No longer fire, just the knowledge of it.

I put it in my pocket.

Lazarus

Martha brings me things I don't need.
The bed is heavy with her cloths.
Basins arrive and depart.
I listen to the soft song of pots and feel her strain.

I dread her questions but also, I want them.
She says *What did you see?* Mary says
Let him rest. I say nothing.

Martha frets at the clamour outside the house.
She says *I killed the cow.*
There is nothing for them.

Mary goes to the door. *Wait* she tells them.
She cuts the shroud into pieces to offer them.
Then they come and I tell them
I stopped but I did not go. Love held me in place.

November

I want to plug my hands into close pockets
and slither in the comfort of weighty coats.

I want hair remembering fire on my pillow
a full measure of night, drenched in black air.

I want to wake, coaxed by light onto my feet
to peer through the draped arms of trees

at the narrowed ambitions of a world
compact as a skull. Now we can offer

the warmth of our bodies as a meaningful gift
let us meet dark change with slowness.

Hanging out with musicians, still in my suit

He said *fucking* and that was important:
"we're all fucking broken."
He said it gently
like a priest, soothing the smart of sin.

I hadn't heard about it before
this shared brokenness
and it was new to me, this idea
that being in pieces could bring us together

so my mind worked through all the things he might mean
and
like the fourteen-stone word association machine that I am
I considered all the world's once-complete, now-shattered things

until I couldn't get it out of my head
that we were broken *like jigsaws*
fucking broken like fucking jigsaws
and it felt right and wise and true.

I ran

for sixty hours that winter
through streets not made for running
over cobbles
hurdling dog leads
choking on cold air and car smoke
muttering at blameless obstacles
raising desperate hands at strangers
slipping on mulched leaves and dogshit
getting up, carrying on
getting faster
fighting bastard hills with nothing but fury and old fat limbs
breathing out like punctured bellows
fucking hell, fucking hell, fucking hell
a fucking hell made
of rasped lungs and lactic and nothing worse.

In Spring we open, like terrifying flowers

I want wild light without people.
I want to escape the places roads pass through.

I want to wake in a forgetful stupor
and fill my empty head with new and reckless thoughts.

When I return to the city
I want people to see me and call my name, ask where I've been.

I am writing this in the bathroom because I can't face saying
that my love is hungrier than I ever told you
in case you say the same
and I am smaller than the ambition of your year.

Wasters

1.

We haze into the day
like the slow smell
of gorse

we jumble together
like cloth magnets

we are offered limbs
soft gravity
clumsy elation.

2.

We're dressed but late and not sorry.
The Gods are proper pissed off.

They give us destinies.
They give us children and paperwork.

3.

When we meet again
it's a hundred years.
My body is no-one's good news.

You are still beautiful.
You hold back.
Do I look that frail?

Waking

I dreamt that we were older. It didn't matter at all.
I was deaf and my balance was poor.
I couldn't smell the flowers. The warm grass
brought me out in hives. Your skin
was patterned. I loved it so much.
I proved it with kisses.
Our voices quavered but when they found clear notes
we felt the magic of it. There was nothing
to be coy about. Sometimes
we broke off, laughing because something ached.
We spent so much time in each other's eyes
that I learnt your face
properly. I named a new sense
and it swallowed the other five:
the sense of you, overwhelming everything.

I wake to the curl of you, the rise of breath.
Everything is paused.
At the window, there is proof of morning
but even now, the alarms are quiet.
You're asleep, or pretending.
You are peaceful and hot. My hair
crunches into you and you turn
as if you had been waiting.
I hope we will be slow.

Saved

We've walked fifteen miles.
It was meant to be ten but the map broke.
Our phones are no use.

We are on a rise. Our legs ache.
The ground is a sump and the tussocks
distort our ankles. Birds cry to their young

that the day is sinking
and must be abandoned.
The moon swims in the late blue

and the heart sings but mostly with fear.
Then, above the grassy loaf
we see orange light, hear sounds

raucous and human. Hands gather us in.
Drinks are pressed on us. Bows are drawn
and fiddles soar. Our hands are seized –

boots give the rhythm. Later, we'll admit
it was not *exactly* like this. For example
we walked only a few steps up the street.

But before that, we decide
that in all important respects
it was.

When the light reminds you to look

On a day like this
when the light is grace

when the light reminds you to look
for grace in yourself

you open the email
from your solicitor

you read the news
you run for the departing bus

you try to talk the world round
you curse, then see

both sides of the choice
and you edit your breath

because it is marvellous
that it still hurts.

Two elephants in a room

When he asked me what I saw
I said *an inkblot*
and because he had had enough
and didn't care anymore
what the ethics committee said
he told me to undress
which I did
and he led me to a mirror.

Now what do you see? he said.
I said *A mirror*

and it was true. I did see a mirror.
I saw what a mirror makes me feel.
I didn't understand it.
I had no use for it.
I have several uses for my body
so, of the two elephants
it was the mirror which stood out
like a bruised appendage.

I was talking with my marvellous man-friend

about our girlfriends with their friends and how it looks so good
the way they laugh together, like a dance you could learn
but not well; and how it's hard sometimes to believe
you could be worthy of time they might spend laughing like that

when I noticed he wasn't talking back. He had a kind of
yes-I've-thought-that-not-exactly-that-but-close-enough look
so I stopped looking for the mercy of regular trips to the bar
and the toilet and looked at him instead. He said

no-one tells you how friendship is a mystery, like love
because that would be to admit that the universe never promised us friends
but sometimes it's a thing you need to say out loud.
So I said yes, it was a mystery, how he was reflecting light

like a seventies space-funk tin-foil pearly king. What light was there
to reflect? It couldn't come from us, because we're extroverts
and our best enemies say we can only drain light from them.
Is it possible that our best enemies are wrong?

The importance of not listening (3)

The world is never lonely. The path
does not need your shoes. Hope
does not need your words. The flake
of moon that slides down your skin
was only looking for a place to rest
the same sun kisses everyone, and the joy
that lifts your feet for no reason
has no reason to it. The sleep you want
absolute but temporary
does not exist, and the home you've found
is a moment, not a tribe. The real you
is often drunk, sometimes cruel
and never gets to the point. Now, ask me:
If that's what you think, why do you smile like that?

House

Come to my house. It is empty.

A prison for sounds.

You can mark it with your footsteps, you can echo in its corners.
There will be time, later, for words.

Before the furniture comes
we can eat pizza from the box and test out the airbed.

Together, we'll make a ghost.

Come in person or in an envelope.
The rules for shoes are *as you please*
and coats go anywhere

but not yet.
Come through here
share with me this little square of sun
say how it will be perfect when I have done
this or that thing which I never will do.

Walk down the hill
buy macaroons and a four pint carry-out
watch clips on my phone.

Just come. Come to my house.
It demands, selfishly
to be filled.

Ashamed of its scuffed bones
ashamed of its honest age
this house is so beautiful naked
I cannot bear it for long.

You and your fridge

To your fridge, you are an idiot God
stashing your milk in its cold gut. Your phone
shares your secrets with the toaster
which scorches the face of your ex onto your bagel
to see if you are paying attention.

Your car comes complete with its own joke. It says
I don't need you anymore. It's true –
you're a legacy organism – but also a consumer
which means your files will be kept
for a long time. On your phone it says

that even after your death they may be conscious.
You blink. The models which describe your behaviour
may be conscious. They will also be
company property. This is not good news.
You stop reading the article. The fridge asks

whether *it* is conscious. You say: *Maybe.*
I don't know. Do you feel conscious?
You blink again, decide what is and isn't real
then you breathe out, like it really means something.
The fridge is silent, perfect, angry, scared.

Home

the bag splits   the fruits spill   enough to fill two hands

we take one each   the skin yields easily   the flesh is sweet

you smile at my busy mouth

on good days   we place the rest in the bowl   next to the occasional flowers

on rare days   our doors open   we tell one truth   *you're welcome*

one lie   *this is how we live*   and our friends seem pleased

I am drinking wine   my mind sticks sometimes   in the wrong places

but I feel   this life   this home   is not wrong

I have noticed that hope   rising   through the mix of things

on the best days   it purrs in my ear   smooth and low

as the throb of a flame in still air   as soft religion   calling

The future, by accident

My daughter woke, desperate to dance
so we kicked and twirled until I was about ready
to puke. Then we said goodbye to the cat
(whose teeth had grown) and stepped out the front door –

into a forest. That's when it came back to me.
Last night! My deal with Death!
One dimension for another. He took east/west
and sealed off all the roads going left and right

from the high street. I got past and future –
a way to move through time with each step.
We must've lost track of the direction of our feet
while dancing, I thought, and travelled back

to when this was all trees. It's common sense
that time flows downhill, so we took the path
of least resistance, waiting for clearings to widen,
watching for crude gutters running with filth

and loads riding on narrow backs above dirt roads.
But the forest went on, muffling the flares
of the sun, and when night came we mulched down
into our own darkness, softening in the late earth.

Thank you

My consolation for baldness will be a hat –
something old-fashioned and well-worn.
I will lift it for anyone worth trusting
with a flash of naked egg.

I will look beyond myself
into the future
guided by the line of my new brim

until my thought cracks into a henge
of orphaned teeth
creases hatching on my skin.

I want this old age.
How badly I want it
now I am forty-four
and we are

Enemies of the People
Saboteurs who need Crushing

and my daughter
still young enough
to reach for my hand when we cross the street.

What I demand of life
is that it go on.

When I am ready
I'll hold my hat to the slosh of my belly
in memory of myself

tilt my head back
bathing my face in the first warm lull
of the morning

and say that one thing
I will finally know I was put here to say.

Catastrophe

Catastrophe lives at the end of the street
in a house the flames get to play in.
Our eyes look back as we quicken our feet.
Catastrophe lives at the end of the street
a glamour no-one is eager to meet
a truth that doesn't want saying.
Catastrophe lives at the end of the street
in a house the flames get to play in.

Acknowledgements and Thanks

Many thanks to all those who have published these poems or earlier versions of them.These include the periodicals *Amaryllis, And Other Poems, Atrium, Butcher's Dog, Clear Poetry, The Fat Damsel, I Am Not A Secret Poet, Ink Sweat and Tears, The Lake, Magma* and *Prole*; and the anthologies *No Tribal Dance* (Angry Manifesto, 2017), *One For The Road* (smith|doorstop 2017) and *The Very Best of 52* (Nine Arches 2015). Several of the poems previously appeared in my pamphlet *Complicity* (smith|doorstop 2016). 'Underground' and 'A Man's House Catches Fire' were published on the Poetry Can website having been respectively placed 2nd and commended in the 2018 Bristol Poetry Prize.

Poetry depends on poets who have used some of their own creative energy to create platforms for others. I would like to thank: Jeremy Toombs especially, for hosting around 400 editions of the Arts House Open Mic where I performed my first poems and began to think of myself as a poet; Andi Langford-Woods and the Acoustic Night team; Jo Bell and Norman Hadley for the 52 project; Carol Ann Duffy and the Poetry Business for *Complicity*; Danny Pandolfi and Lucy English for the Lyra Festival, and Jane Commane for believing in and shaping this book.

My biggest debts are to the people who have been there throughout the period in which these poems were written: my friends Leilah, Adrian, Sarbani and Dave; and most of all Carly, Bethan and my parents. This is your book. I hope you like it.